PRAYER

Clearly See God's Plan For Your Journey

DOWNIE CRAIG

Unless otherwise indicated, all scripture quotations taken from the New American Standard Bible®, copyright ©1960, 1962, 1963, 1968, 1971, 1972, 1973, 1975, 1977, 1995 by the Lockman Foundation. Used by permission.

Scripture taken from The Holy Bible, New International Version®, NIV® Copyright ©1973, 1978, 1984, 2011 by Biblica, Inc.® Used by permission. All rights reserved worldwide.

Scriptures marked NKJV are taken from the New King James Version®. Copyright © 1982 by Thomas Nelson, Inc. Used by permission. All rights reserved.

Scriptures marked KJV are taken from the King James Version (KJV): King James Version, public domain.

Scripture quotations are marked from The ESV Bible (The Holy Bible, English Standard Version®), copyright © 2001 by Crossway, a publishing ministry of Good News Publishers. Used by permission. All rights reserved.

Scripture quotations marked NLT are taken from the Holy Bible, New Living Translation, copyright ©1996, 2004, 2007 by Tyndale House Foundation. Used by permission of Tyndale House Publishers. Inc., Carol Stream, Illinois 60188. All rights reserved.

Scripture quotations marked AMPCE are taken from the Amplified Bible, Classic Edition, Copyright © 1954, 1958, 1962, 1964, 1965, 1987 by The Lockman Foundation. Used by permission.

ISBN: 979-8-218-27369-9

To my late mother,
Cora Johnson Daniels for her love, strength, instruction, and prayers that covered me throughout my childhood, and travel with me now as a mother and grandmother.

I pray many will come to know and fulfill their God-Given vision and journey, through prayer.

CONTENTS

Introduction

God could have spoken to me at any time during my life's journey. He used my mother's death as the catalyst for birthing my vision. While I flew all over the world as a flight attendant, I did not realize how dependent I was on my mother, even into adulthood. He had to break me from that misplaced dependency. My grief triggered a prolonged period of neglect toward my children, and I began a dark, spiraling descent into chronic depression. It was during that dark time that I encountered God and found my purpose in life—the journey to my God-given vision.

Six months after my mother died, I was still grieving. During my bereavement, I had to be hospitalized for a major operation. From there, I lost my appetite. My body weight reduced to a life-threatening sixty pounds.

Late one night, I laid all alone in my hospital bed sleepless and staring at the ceiling in the dimly lit room. My family had gone home. Everything was quiet, except for the soft drone of hospital machines and the occasional patter of the night nurse making her rounds on the ward's cold, white corridors. I began to have my first personal conversation with God. It was difficult to keep any food down, and the doctors were worried about my recovery. In the darkness, I began to cry out to Him, "God, if You are the God You say You are, can You help me stop throwing up and give me my appetite back?" As I cried out silently from the depths of my soul, I suddenly remembered that my mother had once said that if there was any scripture that I should always remember it was the twenty-third Psalm.

I began to speak it, *"The Lord is my Shepherd,"* and God stepped in during that midnight hour. I cannot explain what came over me, but the next day, I began to eat as I recited the Psalm repeatedly. For every spoonful of the warm, nourishing soup, I spoke a part of Psalm 23. I gulped the Word of God to feed my spirit like the huge gulps of food that fed my body.

My deep sorrow continued, and the doctors began a regimen of anti-depressants. One pill turned to two, and two pills turned to five. I realized that my mother had been my dependency, and with her passing, I needed a substitute. Anti-depressants, prescribed by a doctor, became that substitute. I exchanged one dependency for another.

I loved being in the darkness in my room. The drapes in my bedroom were kept closed to keep out any light as I wallowed in self-pity and despair. When my sisters from Louisiana came to visit, things slowly began to change. They entered the bedroom and gently opened the drapes. One of them sat on the side of the bed and looked at me lovingly, but sternly, "Do you want your children to be raised by another woman? Don't you realize while you are grieving for your mother, your children are grieving for theirs?" The realization jolted me out of my stupor. My family was suffering. I selfishly longed for my mother while denying my children the joy and life of their own mother. This moment was the time that I surrendered and confessed that I needed help. I asked God to show me the reason why I was on this earth. This very dark place suddenly became covered with light, and I began to see. The vision for my life was birthed out of my darkest hour. A few days later, I admitted myself to a healthcare facility.

I was scared, but I planned to be there for seven days. All I had was seven days' worth of clothing and my Bible. When I walked in, I heard the Father say to me, "This is the beginning. I am preparing you for your God-given vision." This phenomenon was no psychotic episode because I was balanced on medications. I knew God the Father, was truly speaking.

Everyone there was a stranger to me, but in those seven days, they became real people with real-life situations. I began to pay close attention. I watched as we met in groups. I listened as they told their stories.

I remember having a conversation with one of the patients. He asked if I knew why he was there. He did not expect an answer; he just needed to talk. He explained that, after a heated argument between him and his son, his son committed suicide. Lurching into deep despair and guilt, he ended up in the facility. This gentleman had observed me reading my Bible and talking to God every day. He curiously wanted to know why I was there and why I was reading the Bible daily. He had not socialized with anyone there before, but my actions had caught his attention.

I prayed to the Father, asking Him to give me the words to comfort the gentleman. This was my first intercession. During my brokenness, God was changing my focus from me to this hurting and broken man. The Father said to me, "This is where it begins. You love to talk to people and get involved with their problems. Now, what I want you to do is to troubleshoot for me." My ministry, *Troubleshooting for Christ,* was born.

I began a Bible study in the facility. God had started my ministry right then and there. Another patient who had an eating disorder conversed with me. I could identify with her situation. God said, "Troubleshooter, you know what works. Give her the twenty-third Psalm." I shared my testimony with her and walked her through the same experience that had me eating again. We ate together, and with every bite of food, I quoted a verse from the twenty-third Psalm. God said, "Troubleshooter." I said, "Yes Sir." He replied, "Good job."

Within seven days in the facility, I had become the voice for the group. I was the one God used to set realistic goals for my co-patients. God even used me to minister to the counselors. During a dark gloomy place, God was birthing a vision.

On day seven, I asked everyone on the floor if they wanted to be set free. I wish I could remember the date and the hour that I left – or rather when we left. All the patients on that ward left together at the end of my seven days there. I had experienced miracles, signs, and wonders.

My vision and mission—*Troubleshooting for Christ*—began with a personal crisis followed by a journey of prayer, my secret prayer, a private cry to the Lord in the depths of the night.

Can you see how all this relates to prayer and the journey of finding your God-given vision? I believe that God-given visions begin with a personal and private conversation with God. Prayer is the key to connecting with your God-given vision.

My experience as a flight attendant involved assignments, checking in, meeting with the crew, getting the manifest, and knowing how many passengers were on the flight. It required waking up on the West coast in the morning and going to bed on the East coast in the evening after long intercontinental flights. My preparation— packing the proper clothing and maintaining a positive outlook—must take into consideration different climates, delays, inadequate food services, and inebriated or disruptive passengers. Never once was I fearful about the pilots' qualifications, even though for some it was their first time flying commercially.

In the same way, we must check in with God to know where we are going. We may not know the crew or passengers before starting the journey, but we must trust what God has assigned us to do. We obey because of our trust in God. We know Him as our Father. We know Him as Lord. We know Him to be trustworthy as we build a personal relationship with Him through *prayer*.

As you embark on this journey of prayer, you will discover and interact with your God-given vision. As you read through this book, the Lord God may or may not immediately reveal His vision for your life and that is okay! This book is meant to be read more than once. This journey will be exciting yet challenging.

Your God-given vision will cause you to think, to make choices that only you and God will know about, to spend countless hours with God the Father, and to build a relationship like none other. There will be times when you will know that you have heard from God and times when you will wonder if He is listening to you at all. There will be times of excitement and times of disappointment. There will be times of abundance and times when you must trust Him for your daily bread. There will be questions with and without answers. There will be times when people share your excitement and times when those same people do not understand you.

Praying through the God-given vision is the interaction you will have with God to receive instructions for your vision. You must remember that this is *your* journey. It is just you and your God, the Father. Take time alone with Him daily to receive your instructions. Listen to Him! Talk to Him! The practice of personal prayer will help you to recognize His voice. Remember, you are not alone on the journey, and He is leading you.

Let's begin by asking the Father: *"Father, You said that, if I lacked wisdom and direction, I need to ask You, 'Father, why was I created? What was I created to do for You? What is my purpose here on earth? What are the plans You have for me? Where are You leading me?' Father, I desire to serve You with all my strength, all my soul, and all my spirit for Your glory and pleasure."*

Now pray to the Father: *"Father, Jeremiah 29:11 says the plans You have for me are part of Your vast and infinite knowledge. You said they are good plans, plans for my welfare, my completeness, my peace of mind. You said that your plans are not to bring calamity, injury, or evil but to give me a hope and a future. Your Word in Ephesians 2:10 says that I was created anew in Christ Jesus to do good works, which You planned before I was even born. Psalm 139 says that every moment of my life was laid out before one of them came to be. You made me with great intricacy and skill, carving out my own personality, skills, and talents necessary to live out Your plans. Your thoughts for me are vast and precious. Father, I want to know Your plans—the plans that You were so careful to prearrange for me. You promised in Psalm 138:8 to accomplish and to perfect everything that concerns me, so show me the vision for my life in Jesus's name. Amen.*

Pray for the Vision

Establishing a Personal Relationship with God

But you, when you pray, go into your room, and when you have shut your door, pray to your Father who is in the secret place; and your Father who sees in secret will reward you openly.

Matthew 6:6 NKJV

The airline industry is in the business of helping people reach their destinations. They provide the vehicles, the equipment, and the means by which people move between cities, countries, and continents. In over twenty years as a flight attendant, pilots changed, co-workers changed, cities changed, but every trip started with a plan that began behind the scenes. Complex combinations of flight manifests include a massive coordination of equipment, flight crews, ground crews, and air traffic controllers that are geared towards one thing: helping people accomplish their personal and business travel goals.

Passengers are oblivious to the massive operation that takes place daily. Nothing happens for them until the passenger connects with the airline through a personal call or a visit to the airline's website. All trips begin with a vision, a desire to go on a journey to accomplish a specific purpose.

God works behind the scenes preparing complex manifests for the lives of millions. It is an intricate dance of connections, people moving in and out of our lives—flight crews, ground crews, ground transports—as He moves us along our journey. He has the vision, and we have the need to find purpose. We connect to the vision through *prayer*.

Personal Prayer Requires Privacy

Jesus instructs us to go away by ourselves when we pray. The Life Application Bible translation puts it more directly: we are to go away by ourselves and shut the door behind us. Another translation says, "Go into your private room." While there are many instances in the Bible where we see God's people engaging in corporate prayer (praying collectively in unity), we usually find that all the great men of God—Abram, Moses, the prophets—connected with powerful visions through their personal and private times with God. Jesus gives us many examples of personal prayer's privacy (Matthew 14:23; Mark 6:46; Luke 6:12). For His greatest mission on earth—His Passion—Jesus prepared Himself through personal prayer:

Matthew 26:36

"Then Jesus came with them to a place called Gethsemane, and said to His disciples, 'Sit here while I go over there and pray.'"

At this point, Jesus reduced his prayer partners to His closest disciples—Peter, James and John (Matthew 26:37)—separating Himself from the crowd. But even this separation was not personal enough. He then instructed His closest friends and inner core of disciples to stand back and keep watch.

Matthew 26:38

"Then He said to them, 'My soul is deeply grieved to the point of death; remain here and keep watch with me.'"

Jesus's disciples were expected to support Him. They were instructed to "remain here." In other words, remain here while I go there. They were to be watchful, ever on the alert. They were expected to provide coverage and protection during His personal prayer. Notice, however, they were not invited into this most personal place and time with the Father.

Prayer Is Secret

Matthew 26:39

"And He went a little beyond them, and fell on His face and prayed, saying, 'My Father, if it is possible, let this cup pass from me ... '."

Jesus excused Himself and went a little further away from the disciples, a little beyond them, to be alone with His Father. This movement is an example of prayer's individual nature. This prayer is a type in which there is no intercession and no mediation. It is direct, firsthand, intimate, and confidential. It becomes *secret prayer*. No one else can travel with you beyond this point in prayer. It is customary and biblical for us to request prayer from the elders. According to James 5:16, we are admonished to pray for one another.

Still nothing is sweeter or more profound than entering that most holy and intimate place with God, the Father. In this most secret place—the Holy of Holies, the innermost place—all our secrets are laid bare and welcomed before God. It is also the place where God reveals His secrets to us for profound, life-transforming results.

Jesus modeled this type of prayer as the occasion to validate God's purpose in His life on earth. According to Matthew 26:39, although Jesus requested that God take the bitter cup away, He became entirely focused on God's will. His vision was refreshed, renewed, and refocused to the joy that was set before Him—the higher and enduring purpose of the salvation of the world and the glory of the Father.

Prayer Is Emotional, Physical, and Spiritual

Physical posture characterized Jesus's prayer. According to the Gospel of Luke in the Garden of Gethsemane, Jesus *knelt down,* He bowed the knee and began to pray (Luke 22:41), an act of reverence before the Father. Matthew's account tells us that He *fell on His face* to render worship and homage. This account is a stronger rendering of surrender to His Father. As one who engaged in effective prayer, Elijah has an honorable mention in the Book of James. He undertook an interesting posture as he prayed for rain: "...he crouched down on the earth and put his face between his knees." (1 Kings 18:42).

Jesus's prayer resulted in intense emotions. Read the passages in Matthew 26:38-39 and Luke 22:41-44 to note Jesus's emotional levels. His soul was deeply grieved and distressed to the point of death. He was in agony, engulfed in sorrow. The Message translation expresses the pain like this: *"This sorrow is crushing my life."* Jesus was so emotionally charged that *"his sweat became like drops of blood."* Two psychological conditions occur here that manifest physically or biologically. Through the Spirit, He cried out, *"My Father,"* engaging His Heavenly Father in the moment of deepest anguish. He was making a plea from earth to Heaven. He taught His disciples to pray and address the Father who is in Heaven. This distinction is intentional and motivational because it forces us to realize God's sovereignty and our lowliness. We are challenged to see that God's perspective is vastly different from our own. Prayer motivates us to humility and reverence as we approach the Father.

Prayer Is Relational

Prayer initiates and maintains a personal relationship with God, *your Father*. Relational means the way in which two or more people or things are connected. Matthew 6:6 highlights the relational aspect of prayer. Jesus uses a possessive pronoun when He instructed His disciples to *"pray to your Father."* Prayer is personal not only to you but also to God, the Father.

Connectedness is one of the ways we measure how close people are in a relationship: that is how we determine the functional level of families and marriages. Our relationships meet some specific need or needs in our life. Even our relationship with God can be a need-based relationship. A relationship that adds value is nurtured through closeness, connectedness, intimacy, and trust. This relationship is the kind that God desires to have with us. This relationship is the kind that we see between Jesus and the Father. They are so closely connected that they operate as one. He prayed that we would have this same oneness that He shared with the Father.

John 17:21

"...that they may all be one; even as You, Father, are in Me and I in You, that they also maybe in Us...."

Jesus said these words while in prayer to the Father. He invites us to this level of relationship with the Father through a cultivation of personal and intimate prayer. Prayer is attractive to God. We all desire to remain attractive to our loved ones, especially our spouses.

Personal, relational prayer attracts our Heavenly Father to us. Jesus said that, when we shut ourselves away to talk to the Father, *"then Your*

Father sees" He becomes watchful and attentive to us. This moves Him to respond and take necessary actions. Our personal attention to the Father gets us a personal audience with Him.

Prayer Is a Conversation with God

Prayer is not a monologue but a dialogue. In a dialogue, persons are, '*dia*', across from each other and, '*legein*', exchanging words. This is the same as having a conversation that means 'living with', 'keeping company with', or 'moving towards'. Those in the conversation are together, turning towards each other. We often pray asking God to turn His face towards us.

Our conversation with God may include clarifying questions. Abram exchanged words with God and needed clarification on the promises God was making to him. God promised Abram a great reward. Abram responded, "O Lord God, what will you give me since I am childless...?" (Genesis 15:2). God informed Abram of the land he is going to possess, and Abram inquired, "O Lord God, how may I know that I will possess it?" (Genesis 15:8).

Our conversation with God may include negotiations. On learning that God was about to destroy Sodom and Gomorrah, Abram immediately entered into negotiations with God to save the twin cities. (Genesis 18:16–33).

Prayer Is the Key to Unlocking God's Secrets

When God was about to destroy Sodom and Gomorrah, the habit of conversing between Him and Abram was so well established that God said, *"Shall I hide from Abraham what I am about to do?"* How does it feel to know that you have access into the heart of God? Jesus told His disciples that they have access to the secrets of the kingdom. Clearly, their relationship with Jesus made the difference.

Luke 8:10 NIV

"He said, 'The knowledge of the secrets of the kingdom of God has been given to you, but to others I speak in parables, so that, "though seeing, they may not see; though hearing, they may not understand."'"

In this passage, it is clear that not everyone has the privilege of understanding when God speaks. Only those in a special personalized relationship with God will truly understand when He speaks.

Prayer Is Supernatural

Prayer is a supernatural, transcendental experience between you and God. Just think about it! You are praying to the Father whom you cannot see. For our biblical ancestors, praying to God in Heaven was as natural as having a conversation with a friend. Jesus told the disciples to pray to the Father in Heaven. Somehow, this command did not seem strange to them. This instruction was not met with any protest or challenge. There was sufficient history in the Jewish experience to know that prayer was a supernatural connection with heavenly realms that accomplished great feats on the earth.

Prayer Is Rewarding

Earlier we learned that, in his private and personal conversation with God, Abram was promised a very great reward. God spoke to Abram secretly and rewarded him openly. When we think of reward, we tend to focus on material things, but God's rewards are not limited to just the material things.

God rewards us with peace. The first thing God seeks to do in our lives as a reward is to banish anxiety and frustration. He rewards us by exchanging our anxieties for His peace.

Philippians 4:6-7 NKJV

Be anxious for nothing, but in everything by prayer and supplication, with thanksgiving, let your requests be made known to God; and the peace of God, which surpasses all understanding, will guard your hearts and minds through Christ Jesus.

After my mother's death, I struggled with sleeplessness. The medications the doctors had given me to alleviate the depression were muscle relaxants, and without them, I was unable to sleep. Without them, I would tremble at times. I began to talk to God about bringing peace into my life. In the midst of me talking to God about peace, the trembling stopped. All the things I felt I needed the medication to do were replaced with supernatural peace. God rewarded me with His relaxant. Another side effect of the medication was memory lapses. With my memory restored, I was able to think clearly and make sound decisions. It was also beneficial to my relationships. My laughter, my joy, and my peace were restored.

God rewards us with sound thinking. Before God can begin to show us where He is taking us, He has to help us strengthen the emotional and spiritual weaknesses in our lives. God promises to protect our hearts and our minds. The word 'guard' means to keep watch like a military sentinel. The sentinel's role is simply to make close observation. God sets up spiritual surveillance over our hearts and minds. He deploys whatever defensive and offensive means are necessary to protect the way we think.

God is our reward. It is easy to want material or natural things as rewards. After sharing the vision of blessing with Abram in Genesis 12, God—promising to be Abram's reward—returns to converse with Abram. But Abram questions God about an heir. This reaction in our prayers to God is a natural and human one. We want something that is tangible; yet, in the account of Abram's faith in the Book of Hebrews, we learn that Abram matured to understand God's revelation as the ultimate reward. In spite of tangible, physical rewards that were promised to Abram—a land, a child, and a blessing to all nations—Abram's vision transcended earthly possessions. He began to see a heavenly vision: a city whose foundations, architect, and builder was God Himself.

Hebrews 11:8-10

By faith Abram, when he was called, obeyed by going out to a place which he was to receive for an inheritance; and he went out, not knowing where he was going. By faith he lived as an alien in the land of promise, as in a foreign land, dwelling in tents with Isaac and Jacob, fellow heirs of the same promise; for he was looking for the city which has foundations, whose architect and builder is God.

God rewards us with a clear vision. As Abram continued his time of personal prayer with God in Genesis 15, he was rewarded with a clear vision of what God intended for his life. It is with this clarity of vision that Abram believed God and received the reward of righteousness.

How good it is to know that we can anticipate divine transfer, clarity, and blessing as a result of our prayer. We can anticipate God will reward us, even in our secret and personal time of prayer.

Pray the Vision Worksheet

Prayer Self-Assessment

Think about the most personal relationship that you have. List some of the things you do to maintain this relationship.

1.
2.
3.

Think about your relationship with God. In what ways is your relationship similar to or different from the one above?

1.
2.
3.

What may be happening in your life right now that would drive you to greater personal prayer?

_____

_____

_____

_____

_____

_____

Check the box that best indicates your response to the statements below.

	Never	Seldom	Sometimes	Most Times	Always
I have time set aside for daily prayer					
I pray at least 15 minutes per day					
I tell others my problems before I go to God in prayer					
I believe God speaks to me during my times of personal prayer					
I pray for God to show me my purpose					

God Shares the Vision

Hearing God's Voice

The word of the LORD came to me, saying....

Jeremiah 1:4, 10

G od uses several methods to communicate with us personally. In Scripture, dreams and visions play a crucial role in communicating the will of God for individuals, for His people, and for nations. God communicated to His prophets and people through visions, dreams, and epiphanies. At times, God appeared in physical forms (Numbers 12:8), or angelic beings represented Him. Other times, God used the elements to indicate His presence. At times, the audible voice of God was heard. Other times, supernatural events and acts in nature were manifestations of His purpose and will.

Numbers 12:6-8 NLT

And the LORD said to them, "Now listen to what I say: If there were prophets among you, I, the LORD, would reveal myself in visions. I would speak to them in dreams. But not with my servant Moses. Of all my house, he is the one I trust. With him I speak face to face, clearly and not in riddles; he sees the form of the LORD."

God may impart His will and purpose to us in visions, in dreams, or face to face like Moses. The prophet Joel promised that dreams and visions will be evidence of the manifestation of the Spirit in the last days (Joel 2:28).

Visions

Visions are experienced while we are fully awake. The Word of God came to Abram in a vision in Genesis 15:1. In this vision, an absolutely lucid and coherent conversation took place between God and Abram. The audible voice of God often accompanied the biblical examples of visions.

Dreams

Dreams take place while we are asleep. In the Book of Job, dreams are also called visions of the night.

Job 33:15 NLT

He speaks in dreams, in visions of the night, when deep sleep falls on people as they lie in their beds.

Biblical stories speak of men falling into a deep sleep. Abram's vision in Genesis 15:1 continued with a dream. Here, God caused a deep sleep to overcome him before God disclosed the plans He had for Abram (Genesis 15:12). Jacob encountered God's purpose for him in a dream (Genesis 28:12-15). Job's friend, Eliphaz, received a word from God during a night of deep troublesome sleep.

Job 4:12 NIV

"A word was secretly brought to me, my ears caught a whisper of it, amid disquieting dreams in the night, when deep sleep falls on men."

The prophet Samuel received a word from God during a night vision regarding the deposition of King Saul (1 Samuel 15:10, 16). God also used a night vision to give Daniel the interpretation of Nebuchadnezzar's dream (Daniel 2:19).

Epiphanies

Paul spoke of having a vision and not being sure whether he was in the body or out of the body. This is usually referred to as an epiphany, a moment of sudden revelation or insight.

26

2 Corinthians 12:1b-2 NLT

"... I will reluctantly tell about visions and revelations from the Lord. I was caught up to the third heaven fourteen years ago. Whether I was in my body or out of my body, I don't know—only God knows."

God Provides Clarity for the Vision

We can be certain that God can give us clarity about the vision. God provided very specific instructions to Adam and Eve about their purpose on earth. Noah received this same command after the flood.

Genesis 1:28a; 9:1 NIV

God blessed them and said to them, "Be fruitful and increase in number; fill the earth and subdue it."

Abram received directions to leave his homeland. He learned of God's future plans for himself and his offspring (Genesis 15:4, 5). God said that He spoke clearly to Moses, not in riddles (Numbers 12:7). Jesus told His disciples that the understanding of parables is given to them. We know that the role of the Holy Spirit in the believer's life is to interpret the will of God; He searches the deep things of God, and God reveals the deep and hidden things through His Spirit (1 Corinthians 2:10).

Daniel 1:17

As for these four youths, [Daniel, Hananiah, Mishael, and Azariah,] God gave them knowledge and intelligence in every branch of literature and wisdom; Daniel even understood all kinds of visions and dreams.

27

God Provides Details of the Vision

Visions may provide specific details about what God is doing. During Abram's vision and dreams, there is a personal interaction between God and Abram. God reveals specific details about Abram's posterity. Abram received insight into his future generations. The vision, which God gave to Abram, covered several hundred years. Notice that Abram's visions addressed questions of who, what, when and where. God revealed that Abram would have a son. God provided details about Abram's descendants and that they would be enslaved. God gave specific timelines for certain events to take place.

Paul received his travel plans to Macedonia on his second missionary journey by way of a night vision or a dream (Acts 16:9). Visions may not provide the whole picture. Usually, what God gives us in a vision is just a small part of what He is doing so that we can trust Him to take care of the rest. However, we must also be willing to do our part.

Daniel 12:8-9 NIV

I heard, but I did not understand. So I asked, "My lord, what will the outcome of all this be?" He replied, "Go your way, Daniel, because the words are rolled up and sealed until the time of the end."

How God Speaks to Us Today

We cannot discount God's use of dreams, visions and epiphanies among modern day believers. Joel tells us that this will happen in the last days; we will have dreams and visions. Still one of the surest ways we can know of God's will and purpose is a *prayerful approach to His Word*. The Psalmist says, "thy word is a lamp unto my feet and a light unto my path." (Psalm 119:105 KJV). This means that the Word of God can provide both general and specific details for the journey upon which we are to embark.

God Shares the Vision Worksheet

<u>Finding Vision Mentors</u>

Chapter 11 of the book of Hebrews lists our Heroes of Faith, great men and women we can use as our Vision Mentors. Choose one of these biblical ancestors to study. You will use their life experience to help you walk through your journey.

Write the name of your Vision Mentor and state the reason for choosing him/her.

I am following the journey of _____ because:

_____

_____

_____

_____

_____

_____

_____

Use your concordance to make a note of all biblical references to your Vision Mentor below.

_____

_____

_____

_____

_____

_____

_____

_____

_____

_____

_____

_____

As you study your vision mentor, answer these questions using the table below:

- How much of the Bible is devoted to their story (chapters/verses)?

- What was their personal vision? What was the bigger vision?

- How many times did they engage God or God's representative?

- What excuses/objections did they give concerning achieving the vision?

- Who were the vision busters in their story?

- What were the emotions that your mentor experienced?

- What was their outlook before and after talking to God?

Biblical References	Vision
Conversations with God	Emotions
Personal Excuses/Objections	External Excuses/Objections/ Obstacles
What was accomplished as a direct relationship to God?	List 5 enduring principles you learned from your Vision mentor's story.

Further Observations About Your Vision Mentor

_____

_____

_____

_____

_____

_____

_____

_____

_____

_____

_____

_____

_____

_____

Write the Vision

Every Word from God is Important

*And the LORD answered me: "Write the vision; make it plain on
tablets, so he may run who reads it."*
Habakkuk 2:2 ESV

Congratulations on reaching this part of your journey! Pull up the anchor and let out the sails. It's time to launch into the deep.

We exist in a world of visions. We may refer to them as plans, programs, blueprints, maps, layouts, wills, testaments, and so on. People who champion new causes and monumental ideas for humanity are often referred to as visionaries. Their motivations and intentions produce a particular outcome and achieve a specific purpose, usually for a common good.

The overarching vision of the world is laid out in Scripture in the Old and New Testaments. More than forty authors, over one thousand five hundred years have documented the vision. The first instruction given to the prophet was to record the Vision.

Document the Vision

Recording the vision is the first important step in validating the vision. The prophet Habakkuk was first instructed to write the vision—that is, to document it, to make a journal, or to have an official record. When you consider all the prophetic books in the Bible, you cannot help but think of vision. We are aware of God's acts in history, His word's fulfillment in history, and what is yet to make history because of the meticulous records of the prophets and their scribes.

Here are a few more examples where the prophets were instructed to write their visions:

Exodus 17:14

Then the Lord said to Moses, "Write this in a book as a memorial and recite it to Joshua, that I will utterly blot out the memory of the Amalek from under heaven."

Jeremiah 36:1-2

In the fourth year of Jehoiakim the son of Josiah, king of Judah, this word came to Jeremiah from the LORD, saying, "Take a scroll and write on it all the words which I have spoken to you concerning Israel and concerning Judah, and concerning all the nations, from the day I first spoke to you, from the days of Josiah, even to this day."

Along with His global Vision, the big '*V*,' God has a personal plan for each of us, the little '*v*.' This vision is His plan for our life and purpose on the earth. As He shares this plan with us, He wants us to record those things that He has told us. The moment of revelation can sometimes be so profound and so impactful that we might say, "I can never forget." Still, other times, the voice of God may be so subtle that we wonder if we had heard it at all. We might find ourselves questioning, "Did God really say this is going to happen? Did God really call me to this mission? Did God really ask me to…?"

What do you believe God is asking you to do now? How has He revealed it to you? What happened to persuade you that it was really the call of God? As you embark on your prayer time with the Father, it may help to have a notebook, a red and a black ink pen. It is important to record His will at the moment of conviction, the exact moment when His Spirit compelled you. Use a red pen to write down what the Father says to you. Use the black pen to record your responses, concerns, and questions.

Dating is necessary to document the vision. Notice that, in the above scripture passages, the prophets mention important dates and people. Isaiah records that in the year King Uzziah died, he saw the Lord. Jeremiah noted the king (Jehoiakim), his kingdom (Judah), and the year he received the word of the Lord (the fourth year of the king's reign). Recording the date is important for validating and providing historical and personal context for the vision. Many critics have tried to disprove the accuracy and relevance of the Bible, but they are unable to deny its historical validity.

Many of us keep a daily journal. Each day is dated, and some of us even record the time of the day. The dating of the vision provides situational and historical relevance: Where was I at the time? What were the personal circumstances in my life? What was taking place in the world around me? For example, someone recording the birth of a new member of the family, or a wedding provides situational relevance and validation of the record. Later, when we begin to doubt or question the reality of the vision, we can find assurance that God really said what He said. Dating creates a personal history with God and the way He works in your life.

Make It Plain

The vision may not be clearly understood, but it must be clearly recorded. I once heard a joke about a man who had a close friend who was a doctor. His friend had moved into a new house and invited him to a housewarming party. The man paid no attention to the hastily scribbled directions on his friend's prescription pad until the date of the party. When he realized he could not understand the information, he had the bright idea to take the note to a pharmacist who promptly returned with a prescription.

Have you ever been in a class taking notes, and when you looked them over, you could not understand what you had written? Perhaps you wrote a note to someone, and they could not understand what you were trying to express. Record it clearly so God can unfold the vision over time.

The Vision Has a Legacy of Purpose

The last phrase in Habakkuk's instruction for handling the vision included a purpose clause: *"that he may run who reads it."* There is a reason why the vision must be recorded. Someone is waiting to take the baton from you to continue the vision.

One of my favorite track and field events in the Olympics is the relay race. Time and time again, we see that speed is not the only thing that is required for this race. The technique in passing the baton can make all the difference to the champions. A bad pass or failing to pass the baton within the designated zone can cause the vision of Gold to shatter like a crashing chandelier.

Jeremiah's careful recording of the vision received from God provided useful information to Daniel many years later to give hope to his people.

Daniel 9:2 NIV

In the first year of his [Darius, son of Xerxes] reign, I, Daniel, understood from the Scriptures, according to the word of the Lord given to Jeremiah that the desolation of Jerusalem would last seventy years.

Very often, we want to own the vision and, if necessary, to die with the vision or have the vision die with us. Whether we like it or not, our vision goes beyond the grave. In the same way, our vision should go beyond us. In other words, it is never only about us.

A small group leader at my church shared a story with me. One group member warned at the beginning of the very first group meeting that she may not come back after that first visit. The reason she gave was that she already knew her purpose. I was very saddened by this confession, as she saw no need to share her vision with others. God could be planning on pairing her with someone to help accomplish the vision, but she may miss the opportunity. Her attitude was also selfish, as she did not see the need to encourage others toward fulfilling their vision.

The Vision Has a Legacy of Preparation

Isaiah 62:10 NIV

Pass through, pass through the gates! Prepare the way for the people. Build up, build up the highway! Remove the stones. Raise a banner for the nations.

Our vision may be paving the path for others to follow. The experiences that we have and the path that is charted create a sense of comfort for those coming after us. They are doors and gates that our vision will provide; gates that will allow others to follow. Moses passed the baton to Joshua. Eli prepared Samuel. Zerubbabel guided the exiles and began the rebuilding of the temple. Ezra continued by adorning the temple, and Nehemiah followed by rebuilding the walls of Jerusalem. While they all shared a common vision, they still had different roles to play concerning the vision of a reconstructed temple. The recorded visions of Abram told the Israelites that they would be enslaved for four hundred years. The informed visions of the Major Prophets alerted God's people to the duration of their exile, the rise of a pagan king to facilitate their release, and the blessed hope of the coming Messiah. God's people knew what they could anticipate in the future because of the recorded visions of the prophets.

And consider the Roman Roads, an intricate network radiating in all directions from the central command in Rome. The Roman legions traveled quickly, as much as twenty-four miles on this road system in one day, carrying heavy military assault weapons and supplies. They conquered a vast number of regions. These roads played an integral role in accelerating the spread of the Gospel to the ends of the earth. While the world seemingly went into a period of spiritual darkness for four hundred years, God prepared for the Light of the World to make His appearance on earth and the ultimate vision of salvation for all peoples of the world.

10 TIPS FOR PREPARING TO
WRITE THE VISION

1. Always keep a notebook nearby! You never know when God is going to speak.

2. Be prepared to write anytime of the day, whether early in the morning or late at night. Remember epiphanies can occur at any time.

3. Write something! Even if an idea seems ridiculous to you, write it down to pray about later.

4. RESPOND! Do not ignore God's voice if you hear Him calling you deep in the night.

5. Do not box God in! Do not try to fit Him into your schedule. Let Him set your schedule.

6. The Vision is not yours! You are only the vessel God is using to complete His vision for your life.

7. Be quiet and listen!

8. Find time to be alone with God!

9. Speak out loud to the Father!

10. Share your deepest personal thoughts with God! All the things you may want to tell a close friend, tell it to the Father, for He is your best friend and Redeemer.

Write the Vision Worksheet

Journal the Vision that you believe God has laid on your heart during your personal time with Him.

(It may have been an inspiration that has been dormant since childhood.)

_____

_____

_____

_____

_____

_____

_____

_____

_____

Believe the Vision

Commit Yourself to the Task

Therefore I say to you, whatever things you ask when you pray,
believe that you receive them, and you will have them.

Mark 11:24 NKJV

B elief in the vision requires us to be comfortable, confident, and bold in our requests to God. Jesus tells us that we can receive whatever we ask for in prayer.

2 Corinthians 3:12

*Therefore, having such a hope, we use great **boldness** in our speech.*

Ephesians 3:12 NLT

*Because of Christ and our faith in him, we can now come **boldly** and confidently into God's presence.*

Hebrews 4:16 HCSB

*Therefore, let us approach the throne of grace with **boldness**, so that we may receive mercy and find grace to help us at the proper time.*

Our conviction of our God-given vision gives us boldness. We may confidently approach God when things seem to go contrary to what God has promised. When we feel that we have strayed away from the vision or have attempted to change the vision, we may boldly approach God. He promises grace and help when we find ourselves off-track. God expects us to be bold in approaching His throne of grace, to march confidently into His presence, because we know that He is faithful and just.

Barriers to Belief

In spite of the encouragement, being bold may appear simpler on paper than what you may have experienced in reality. There are many things I have prayed for and still have not received. However, there are legitimate reasons for not receiving answers to our prayers. Here are some of them:

47

1. **Improper requests** — We ask for things that conflict with God's laws and principles.

2. **Disbelief** — We are not convinced of God's plans and promises.

3. **Disobedience** — Delays may be due to our unwillingness to do what God has directed us to do.

4. **The Not-Yet factor** — God has a designated timing for the prayer to be answered.

5. **Demonic interference** — Spiritual warfare delays the response.

One of the basic principles in understanding Scripture is that Scripture interprets itself. Scripture confirms itself. So, let's seek clarity as we further examine the biblical principles concerning the hindrances to answered prayer.

Improper Requests

James 4:3 NKJV

You ask and do not receive, because you ask amiss....

James dispels the notion that we can ask God for anything when the request may be inappropriate. Asking amiss could mean we are asking God for inappropriate things, or we are asking and expecting appropriate things at inappropriate times.

An improper request may also be one that is inconsistent with God's Word. Our requests must line up with God's general principles and laws. It must not contradict His Word in any way, shape, or form, for God only does what is consistent with His Word.

Psalm 80:4

"O LORD God of hosts, how long will you be angry with the prayer of Your people?"

Since our prayers may be inconsistent with God's Word, it is important to examine how we approach God and what we ask for. We must approach God with reverence and humility.

Disbelief

Hebrews 3:12 NIV

See to it, brothers and sisters, that none of you has a sinful unbelieving heart that turns from the living God.

Disbelief is one of the biggest threats to our vision. We often give God excuses why we cannot do something, whether it's our money, education, influence, etc. We find many reasons why we do not believe that He can or would use us. We doubt our own capabilities, seeing ourselves as inadequate. Listen to some of the excuses of our biblical ancestors:

Exodus 4:10

Then Moses said to the LORD. "Please Lord, I have never been eloquent, neither recently nor in the time past, nor since You have spoken to Your servant; for I am slow of speech and slow of tongue."

Jeremiah 1:6

Then I said, "Alas, Lord God! Behold I do not know how to speak, because I am a youth."

God disagrees with these excuses. He said to Moses:

"Who has made man's mouth? Or who makes the mute, the deaf, the seeing, or the blind? Have not I, the LORD? Now therefore, go, and I will be with your mouth and teach you what you shall say." (Exodus 4:11-12 NKJV).

In the Book of Acts, we learn far more about Moses and his capabilities. Having been raised in Pharaoh's house as a grandson, Moses would have received all the great tutoring and grooming in eloquent and persuasive speech.

Acts 7:22 NIV

Moses was educated in all the wisdom of the Egyptians and was powerful in speech and action.

In response to Jeremiah, God says:

"Do not say, 'I am a youth,' For you shall go to all to whom I send you, and whatever I command you, you shall speak. Do not be afraid of their faces, for I am with you to deliver you...." (Jeremiah 1:7-8 NKJV)

In both examples, God is saying that our human limitations are irrelevant to the vision. He not only determines where we go and what we do, but He equips and protects us.

Disobedience

Psalm 66:18 KJV

If I regard iniquity in my heart, the Lord will not hear me.

Have you ever tried to have a conversation with someone who was not listening? How frustrating is that? Earlier we define prayer as an exchange between God and us. We approach God, and He responds to us. At least, that is the expectation.

Perhaps we have not dealt with issues of sin in our own lives. The function of the Holy Spirit is to convict us of sin. We grieve Him when we disobey God's Word (Ephesians 4:30, 1 Thessalonians 5:19).

Anything that grieves the Holy Spirit's work in your life is sin. Disobedience is sin. Disobedience not dealt with, may prevent you from connecting with your vision.

The Not-Yet Factor

An unanswered prayer may not be a 'no' but a 'not yet'. One reason for a not-yet response from God may be our inability to handle something at that particular time. This response may be due to a lack of maturity or a lack of necessary skills and resources.

For example, young children may try to convince you they know how to drive a car. Even if you did allow them to hold the steering wheel, would you allow them to put their feet on the gas pedal, or even drive past your own driveway? Not very likely! While we know that they have the potential to be good drivers one day, there are legal and safety requirements for driving on public roads. They have yet to acquire the logic and motor skills combined with the ability to make decisions at critical moments.

God knows when we are ready to step into active roles for the vision. Jesus often told His disciples, *"My time has not yet come." (John 7:6, 8 NKJV)*. He sets the example of the importance of the time to enact the vision.

There are also gestation periods for vision, periods of time during which the vision is maturing. God told Abram that His people shall return to their promised land after 400 years of enslavement, when the iniquity of the Amorites was completed (Genesis 15:16).

The spread of the Gospel could not have been efficient without the system of Roman roads. During the four hundred years before the birth of Christ, significant world events literally paved the way for the spread of the Gospel.

Another example is the Apostle Paul, who received the vision some fourteen years before beginning his missionary journeys (Galatians 2:1). There is a proper, God-appointed time for the vision. God may call you to leave a successful corporate career to become a missionary or a pastor. However, the calling does not always equate to the timing. You may need to be trained in missions and pastoring.

God may also be preparing a specific ministry posting for you that has not yet become available. As He is equipping you, He is also putting people and resources in place to allow you to fulfill the vision. Our continual secret prayer with God helps to keep us on track with the vision's timing.

Demonic Interference

The demonic principalities intercepted the answer to Daniel's prayer over the region of Persia (Daniel 10:12-13). Even though the prayer had been answered from the time Daniel prayed, he did not experience the answer because of a supernatural conflict. The answer to our prayer and the manifestation or experience of the answer may not happen at the same time.

Beware of Vision Busters

Be on the lookout for vision busters. Some people call them pallbearers. This person is the one who will help you bury your vision. This individual will find all the reasons why your idea is ridiculous or impossible. In contrast, stand with the armor bearer, the one who comes alongside you and supports you in the vision. One example in the Old Testament refers to the armor bearer (or officer) as the one *"whose hand he leaned"* (2 Kings 7:2, 17 NKJV). Their role is to take some of the burden of the task at hand away from you.

God communicated to Joseph through dreams. When Joseph shared his first dream with his brothers, they hated him because of the dream and what he said about the dream (Genesis 37:5-8).

When he shared another dream with his father, he was rebuked (Genesis 37:10). The closest and most important people in Joseph's life dismissed the visions that God was birthing in his life.

Avoid ungodly counsel to facilitate the vision. Saul received instructions during his reign as king of Israel from the prophet Samuel; however, there was a time when he impatiently consulted with a witch. His hasty actions destroyed his vision. He lost the kingdom, he lost his sons, and he lost his life. Sometimes, in our haste, when we think that God has abandoned us, we are tempted to try to assist God. This hastiness may lead to great personal loss.

We now come to another important principle in the vision's journey. Scripture is filled with examples in which belief in God's response was equated with waiting. In other words, it is a matter of time. Many of the passages in the gospels are prefixed with the phrase, 'And it came to pass...' or the phrase, 'This was to fulfill what the prophet said...'. Your vision may be the starting point of a larger vision. It might be that your vision is the continuation of someone else's vision. Remember that, ultimately, the vision belongs to God. We are merely carriers, messengers, and channels of God's plan.

Whatever you do after having cultivated that intimate relationship with God, received the Word of God, written the Word of God down, is to believe that God is able and committed to finish what He has started. Believe that He is working in you to do what pleases Him (Philippians 2:13).

Belief Requires Remembrance

A constant refrain to God's people by the prophets was, "Remember, remember..." There is a good reason why God tells us to "write the vision." Human beings usually have short memories. What God promises in our answers to prayer and the vision, usually involves time so we are apt to forget. A well-documented vision helps us to remember.

One of the things I have practiced in my life is to record my prayers and requests. Very often I go back to inquire of God, noting the date and time I had made the request. The best part of this practice is to have an answered prayer and to look back to see where I was, what was going on at the time, and what things transpired between the prayer and the answer. This practice builds trust.

Belief Produces Confident Prayer

1 John 5:14-15 NKJV

Now this is the confidence that we have in Him, that if we ask anything according to His will, He hears us. And if we know that He hears us, whatever we ask, we know that we have the petitions that we have asked of Him.

In the Lord's prayer, we say, *"Thy will be done in earth as it is in heaven."* (Matthew 6:10 KJV). There is no guarantee that God will honor our will, but we know that whatever He desires comes to pass. Then we can pray confidently, because we are praying the will of the Father and we can expect whatever we ask!

Hebrews 4:16 says we are to approach God in confidence and boldness. Confidence in our prayers is grounded in the understanding that God hears us and that he attends to our petitions. However, if we do not believe that God is doing what He said He can and will do, we should not expect anything from God (James 1:6-8). Sometimes we must bolster our confidence in prayer by reminding ourselves of the attributes of God—His omnipotence, His omniscience, His omni-presence, etc. This is modeled in many prayers in Scripture.

Here are some examples of prayers:

When Jehoshaphat was under attack, He began to call on God by first acknowledging His character and attributes.

2 Chronicles 20:5-6 NIV

Then Jehoshaphat stood up in the assembly of Judah and Jerusalem at the temple of the LORD in the front of the new courtyard and said: "LORD, the God of our ancestors, are you not the God who is in heaven?

You rule over all the kingdoms of the nations. Power and might are in your hand, and no one can withstand you.

When the deliverance of the Jewish exiles from Babylonian captivity was under the threat of failure, Nehemiah prayed, beginning with an appeal to the attributes and the character of God.

Nehemiah 1:5 NIV

"LORD, the God of heaven, the great and awesome God, who keeps his covenant of love with those who love him and keep his commandments...."

When the local Jewish rulers challenged the early church, the believers prayed with acknowledgments of God's creative power and His sovereignty over all of creation.

Acts 4:24 NIV

When they heard this, they raised their voices together in prayer to God. "Sovereign Lord," they said, "you made the heavens and the earth and the sea, and everything in them."

In all these examples, there is some reference to God with His power and influence in the earth, His faithfulness and trustworthiness. There is nothing too difficult for Him. It is impossible to endorse your vision without your confidence in God's power and integrity to perform what He says that He can and will do.

Belief Anticipates Receiving

The next instruction is to believe that you have received what you pray for and that what you pray for will be yours. Now here is where we need to examine the biblical tenses. The first tense speaks of something that has already happened in the past. In the moment that we ask, the moment God has the receipt of our requests, the answer warps into past tense. We are to believe that we have already received what we asked for. And here's the key, we are given a guarantee for the future: *"and it will be yours."* I should believe I already have something that I do not have, cannot see with my physical eye, and sometime in the future it will somehow materialize. That is just how it works according to Scripture.

Many of you have heard stories of people working through their visions with God and coming to some incredibly difficult places. Does that mean the vision is in jeopardy? Not at all! We are simply to believe that God has already covered all the points. He is ahead of us, charting our path. He is a great motivator on the earth, raising valleys and leveling mountains. We must accept that it is already done.

Whatever you do, having cultivated that intimate relationship with the Lord, having received the word of the Lord, having written it down, believe that God is able and committed to finish what He has started. Believe that He is working *in you both to will and to do for His good pleasure. (Phil 2:13 NKJV)*

Here is a quick recap for you. So far, we have learned:

1) Prayer is a personal, intimate, relational exchange between you and the Father. The relationship with the Father makes Him willing to share secrets with you. This means that in your time with Him, your prayer and desires are calibrated to align with His.

2) Your relationship with the Father gives you the confidence that you have indeed heard His voice, know the vision, and therefore can approach Him with confidence and boldness.

Believe the Vision Worksheet

Summary of My Vision	What God Said in My Secret Time with Him.
Scriptures I Will Use to Support My Vision	Emotions
Personal Excuses/Objections	External Excuses/ Objections
What changes are you noticing in your life?	What are you learning about God/ about yourself?

Trust the Vision

Partner with God in Faith

"The LORD said to me, "You have seen well...."
Jeremiah 1:12 NKJV

The Vision Comes with a Provision Clause

Part of God's provision for the vision is the people that he brings into your life to assist you. There will always be others involved in helping you to complete the vision. When God spoke to me about The Kingdom Game, a board game that He called me to develop, I had no experience in developing games. I did not know the graphic artist. I did not know the printing company. I did not know who might be interested in purchasing the product. Although I did not know anything, God surely knew everything. He set up the companies and the people that I needed to be in place.

Be prayerful about who you take along on your journey. Abram brought Lot and experienced family conflict. Lot brought a lot of trouble. But look to God to provide resources.

2 Corinthians 9:10

Now He who supplies seed to the sower and bread for food will supply and multiply your seed for sowing and increase the harvest of your righteousness.

The Vision Comes with a Protection Clause

On his journey to the land that was promised, Abram had to pass through hostile territory. Despite wanting a peaceful passage, he found himself enveloped into the war of the kings of Sodom and Gomorrah, because his nephew, Lot, had been taken captive. Following Abram's victory, God appeared to reassure Abram, to calm any lingering fear and to comfort him with protection.

Genesis 15:1

After these things the word of the LORD came to Abram in a vision, saying, "Do not fear, Abram, I am a shield to you...."

God also promised Jeremiah safe passage.

Jeremiah 1:8, 17 NKJV

"Do not be afraid of their faces, For I am with you to deliver you," says the LORD. "Therefore prepare yourself and arise, and speak to them all that I command you. Do not be dismayed before their faces, lest I dismay you before them."

God's vision for us often takes us through hostile territory. The journey often involves significant risk, and with those risks comes fear. In our above examples, God addresses the fears that they encounter. Both Abram and Jeremiah were afraid of the people for different reasons. In our personal secret time with God, He can comfort and strengthen us through our times of fear.

The Vision Comes with a Performance Clause

Jeremiah 1:12

Then the LORD said to me, "You have seen well, for I am watching over My word to perform it."

God told Jeremiah that He was keeping watch over His word to perform it, to make it come to pass. Remember that God is the one giving the vision. God is the one performing it. He ultimately owns the vision. We are only vessels, vehicles, and conduits through which God performs.

64

Let us reassure ourselves, like the Psalmist David, recognizing that God is the one who retains the obligation to perform His Word and to accomplish His purpose in our lives.

Psalm 57:2 <small>AMPCE</small>

*I will cry to God Most High, who **performs** on my behalf and rewards me [Who brings to pass His purposes for me and surely completes them]!*

Trust God for the Vision Worksheet

Make a list of resources that you will need to carry out the vision.

1.

2.

3.

4.

Make a personal list that you may need to complete for the vision (for example, completion of a course, training, etc.).

1.

2.

3.

4.

Make a list of connections that you may need to establish for support or information (for example, mentors, etc.)

1.

2.

3.

4.

Work the Vision

Putting Your Feet to Your Faith

"...faith by itself, if it is not accompanied by action, is dead."

James 2:17 NIV

Believers make a distinction between saving faith and working faith. In the letter to the Ephesians, Paul declares to the church of Ephesus that we are saved by grace through faith, not of our own actions. Faith comes by hearing the Word. The Greek word for 'hearing the Word' is *rhema,* and it refers to the in-birthing of faith in those who were dead in their trespasses and sins. This type of faith is what is known as saving faith, which affirms the believer's position in Christ.

In the letter from James, we learn that "faith without works is dead." James is addressing a different kind of faith. The practice of faith, or working faith, is different from saving faith. Working faith is the action during the life of a Christian that demonstrates obedience to God. Working the vision requires *working faith.*

An example of working faith is Abram's obedience to God to prepare his son Isaac to be sacrificed. We cringe at what may seem to be a cruel request from God. Even though we know in hindsight that Isaac was saved, we may tend to wonder why God put Abram through such emotional turmoil. It all contributes to our spiritual strengthening.

I personally experienced the fruits of struggle as well. After years of developing the Kingdom game, praying about the direction to take it and how to present it to stores, the Lord God opened the door for the Kingdom Game to be sold in big-box store exchanges, even though I had no previous experience in game development or marketing expertise. Talk about an emotional roller coaster along the way!

Consider this example: even as Jeremiah was prophesying the imminent capture and exile of the Jewish people to Babylon, God was also giving him the vision that the people will eventually return to their land. He instructed Jeremiah to invest in the latter part of the vision by buying a field. Read Jeremiah 32:6-15 to study this example of working faith. In this passage, Jeremiah received a list of instructions that might not have made sense given the hostile geopolitical conflict: (1) buy a field and document the terms and conditions of the purchase; (2) have the document signed and affixed with an official seal; (3) have the transaction witnessed publicly; (4) make a copy; and (5) secure both the original and the copy in a clay jar to preserve them.

There are times when God will ask us to make an investment in the vision. He may ask you to leave your job and go back to school. He may ask you to change your career. In other words, He wants you to put your trust in Him. Faith is when we take certain decisive actions that support the vision in a tangible way. In many cases it places a demand on our personal resources.

Peter said, "Jesus, if it is you, bid me to come." Peter asked for clarity and confirmation before he walked on the water. Jesus provided what Peter needed to take the next step.

After you have prayed, faith will cause you to step out of the boat. Jesus showed Peter it was possible. Jesus was already walking on the water to encourage Peter's faith. Jesus says, "Come." Do you hear Jesus saying that to you?

Faith will cause you to walk on the water when everyone else is still in the boat. Do not be distracted by the people you leave behind. They cannot help you. Keep your eyes firmly ahead and locked on Jesus. Just talk to Him. He has already prepared the way for you.

Tips to Working Your Vision
• Involve the Lord God in every decision: Daily. Hourly. Ask, "What do you want me to do, Lord?" Make sure to obey His instructions.
• Allow the Lord God to be your vision partner: He is the architect of the vision. We are His assistants. Let God lead. He is responsible for making all the necessary plans. Be sensitive to His leading. We are ambassadors for the Lord Jesus Christ.
• Discover ways of working your vision: God allows you to do things only you can do. Tap into unique talents and skills He has given to you. Speak His Word. You were formed in secret by the same God who knows you best. He will instruct you on the "Who? How? When?" Build a track record (journal) of His supernatural interventions.
• Discover ways of putting your faith to work: If you cannot believe it, how will others see it when it's time to 'pitch it'? The testimony is greater when it is just you and God, so that He can get all the glory.
• Picture your vision working and accomplishing its purpose: See it working. What do you have in your hand? What has He given to you? Be teachable. Picture your success. Give Him all the glory.

Vision in Action

Time to Step Out of the Boat

...Pray without ceasing.
I Thessalonians 5:17 NKJV

Pray sincere prayers, "help!" prayers, pray over plans both large and small. Pray for clarity and then listen as you talk with God. Pray angry, pray rejoicing, pray scared, but still pray.

Keep prayer personal and relational. Your best relationship, without exception, is with God. Thank Him daily for that privilege!

Journal the Journey

As you listen for the Lord God to speak to you, write everything you hear from Him. Write down the time, place, and date so you can document your journey. Believe in what you have heard from the Lord God and trust Him wholeheartedly. Half-hearted faith will not carry you to what's next. Step out on faith without wavering. Watch in awe as the Lord God completes the vision.

Encouragement for the Journey

This journey will not be easy. You will stretch, grow, and become stronger in your faith. You will learn to hear God more clearly, trust God more completely, and cling to His Word at all times. My development stages were maturing and preparing me for the next steps. God may be saying, "Do not get comfortable in the boat; I have more for you. This is just the beginning." This is not a pride building adventure. God's vision, seen clearly, will bless others. As John the Baptist said, "He must increase, but I must decrease." (John 3:30 NKJV)

Obedience is required. God has put me in time out for not listening to Him. I have heard Him say, "Let's begin again when you are ready, but not today." Remember, His timing is perfect. There are times during the day when He would prompt me to call someone who I had not been able to reach. I will never know all that God knows, but I listened to Him in obedience.

You will meet all sorts of negative people, including naysayers, betrayers, and liars, but keep on moving. There is no time to have a pity party. God will complete the vision, for His glory. I met vision busters, and you may too, but God still says, "Come. Get out of the boat." This is a shared vision between you and God. He pushed me towards my vision through mourning and recovery. He is the only true multi-tasker who remains 100% faithful to His people, bringing healing and completion on multiple fronts at one time.

Philippians 1:6 KJV

Being confident of this very thing, that he which hath begun a good work in you will perform it until the day of Jesus Christ....

I pray this book will jump start your vision, as God will complete it. Enjoy your journey, in Jesus' name.

An Adopted Family

Joining the Community of Faith

So, you are no longer a slave, but a son, and if a son, then an heir through God.

Galatians 4:7 ESV

Walking, talking, planning and listening to God assumes you have been introduced to God in the first place. Are you saved and adopted into His family?

Salvation

The gift of salvation is easily attainable. The Bible tells us that we all have sinned and fallen short of the Glory of God. (Romans 3:23). However, God has shown us His love by sending Christ to die for us. (Romans 5:8). Christ died so that we can have eternal life, all we have to do is confess with our mouth that Jesus is Lord and believe in our heart that God raised Him from the dead, so that we can be saved. (Romans 10:9-10).

Pray

"Father, I have sinned against you. I ask for Your forgiveness. I believe in my heart that You have raised Christ from the dead. I put my trust in You and confess Jesus Christ as my Lord and Savior. I surrender my life to You, Jesus. Thank You for saving me. In Jesus Name, Amen.

Welcome to the family of faith! Be sure to find a local church where you can grow and serve.

Acknowledgments

I am thankful for all the individuals who contributed their time, talent, and experience in the writing of this book:

To my children and grandchildren, for your kindness, love, obedience, encouragement, and support which has allowed me to fulfill the vision the Father has given to me, I love you and I am blessed to have you.

Downie Craig is the Founder and CEO of Troubleshooting for Christ, Inc. and Heaven Sent Products, LLC.

She has a heart for women to establish themselves as independent, yet family centered, contributing members of society.

Ms. Craig has served widows and their families, abused and battered women, pregnant teens, homeless, and incarcerated women for over 30 years. She brings her extensive Biblical knowledge to her teaching and counseling roles.

Her heartfelt efforts have made a life-changing impact on all who come to know her.

www.downiecraig.com

www.ingramcontent.com/pod-product-compliance
Lightning Source LLC
Chambersburg PA
CBHW030508130626
46549CB00007B/2891